Editor
Torrey K. Maloof

Editor in Chief
Karen J. Goldfluss, M.S. Ed.

Creative Director
Sarah M. Fournier

Cover Artist
Sarah Kim

Illustrator
Mark Mason

Art Coordinator
Renée Mc Elwee

Imaging
Amanda R. Harter

Publisher
Mary D. Smith, M.S. Ed.

TCR 8292

LET'S
DAY GET STARTED
Math

- Start the day off right with engaging standards-based mathematics

- Over 100 pages of activities organized by mathematical concepts, such as counting & cardinality, adding & subtracting, measuring, and geometry

- Activities help improve mathematical reasoning skills and prepare students for real-world problem solving

- Reflection questions conclude each section allowing students to assess their own learning and understanding of mathematical concepts

Teacher Created Resources

Author
Samantha Chagollan

Teacher Created Resources
12621 Western Avenue
Garden Grove, CA 92841
www.teachercreated.com
ISBN: 978-1-4206-8292-2
© 2019 Teacher Created Resources
Made in U.S.A.

Table of Contents

Introduction

Mathematics can be tough for teachers to teach and even tougher for students to learn. Math is not always a fan favorite among the elementary school crowd. It can be intimidating and frustrating. The *Let's Get This Day Started* series is designed to provide students with frequent opportunities to master and retain important math skills in a simple, user-friendly manner.

This book is designed to reinforce key mathematics skills taught in the classroom. As students become active learners in discovering mathematical relationships, they acquire a necessary understanding that improves their problem-solving skills and boosts their confidence in math. When using this book, consider incorporating these activities with the actual curriculum that you may be currently using in your classroom. This provides students with a greater chance of mastering math skills and ultimately being successful in college, career, and life.

The activities in this book do not need to be completed every day or even every other day. Teachers should not feel restricted by a daily warm-up or introductory activity. Sometimes, schedules change. A morning assembly, a make-up lesson, or just an extra-busy day can easily throw off a classroom schedule for days. Teachers never know what their days or weeks are going to look like. This book is written so that teachers can stop wherever and whenever they want. They can take their time and arrange the activities to fit their own schedules. They may choose to do a section a day, or spread it out over a week or two. There is no right or wrong way.

This book is divided into units based on different mathematical-content strands. Each unit consists of sections focused on a topic related to that particular unit. Each four-page section has its own art theme. A whole-class introductory sheet kicks off each section, followed by a paired-learning activity sheet, and then an independent-learning assessment. Each section concludes with a written response to a prompt that incorporates the topic studied in the section.

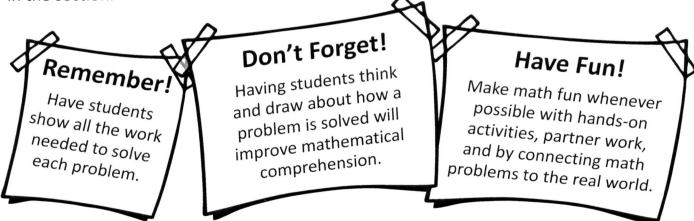

Remember!
Have students show all the work needed to solve each problem.

Don't Forget!
Having students think and draw about how a problem is solved will improve mathematical comprehension.

Have Fun!
Make math fun whenever possible with hands-on activities, partner work, and by connecting math problems to the real world.

All the activities in the *Let's Get This Day Started* series have been aligned to the Common Core State Standards (CCSS). Visit *http://www.teachercreated.com/standards/* for all standards correlations.

How to Use This Book

The first page in each section is the *Look & Learn* page. This page introduces the mathematical topic that will be covered in the section. It breaks down the basics of the mathematical concept by using simple words, diagrams, and examples. This page should be a whole-class activity. The teacher should read and review the page with students aloud, answering any questions they may have. These introductory pages can then be saved in a folder and used as study guides, homework helpers, or cheat sheets.

The second page in each section is the *Partner & Practice* page. This page includes problems for students to solve with a partner. Working collaboratively will provide students with additional guidance and support. Teachers should place students into heterogeneous or homogenous pairs, and circulate around the room as students work together to solve the problems on the page. Teachers should check for understanding and be sure that each student in every pair is actively involved and fully invested in the work. Be sure students show all the work needed to solve each problem. When pairs have finished the page, go over the answers as a class.

The third page in each section is the *Your Turn* page. This page includes problems for students to solve independently. This page can be completed in class or assigned as homework, and can be used to assess student understanding. Again, be sure students show all the work needed to solve each problem. If students struggle to complete the problems correctly, teachers may wish to supplement with additional learning activities and practice.

The fourth and final page in each section is the *Think & Draw* page. This page includes prompts to help students reflect on the mathematical concept and put their understanding of it into drawings. It provides them with opportunities to review, confirm, and reinforce their learning as well as write about how math problems are solved. Students can save these pages and use them to create a math journal to help them review what they have learned throughout the year.

Look & Learn	Partner & Practice	Your Turn	Think & Draw
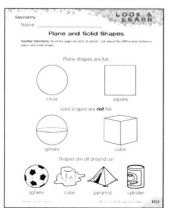	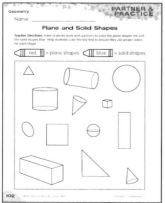	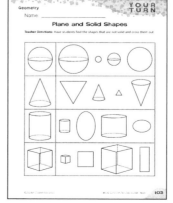	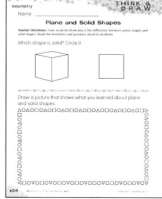

Name: _____

Writing Numbers 1–10

Teacher Directions: Read the page aloud to students. Have students practice tracing the numbers at the bottom of the page.

Let's learn how to write numbers!

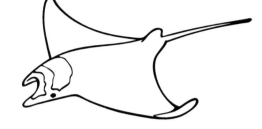

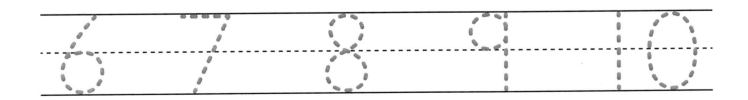

Name: _____

Writing Numbers 1–10

Teacher Directions: Have students trace the numbers at the bottom of the page, cut them out, and then work with partners to glue them in the correct boxes.

Name: _____

Writing Numbers 1–10

Teacher Directions: Have students trace the numbers at the bottom of the page, cut them out, and then glue them in the correct boxes.

    #8292 Let's Get This Day Started: Math   **7**

THINK & DRAW

Name: _____

Writing Numbers 1–10

Teacher Directions: Have students think about the numbers 1–10. Read the directions aloud to students.

Write the numbers 1–10 in order.

_____

- -

_____

- -

_____

Draw 7 fish in the ocean.

Name: _____

Writing Numbers 11-20

Teacher Directions: Say each number aloud with students. Have students trace each number. Then, have students practice writing the numbers on the lines at the bottom of the page.

Let's learn how to write bigger numbers!

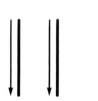  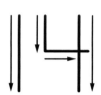 

_____

- -

_____

- -

_____

- -

_____

Name: _____

Writing Numbers 11-20

Teacher Directions: Have students work with partners to count aloud the number of fruit in each row in the first column. Then, have students trace the numbers in the second column and, finally, write the number in the third column.

(apples)	12	
(oranges)	13	
(lemons)	14	
(pears)	15	

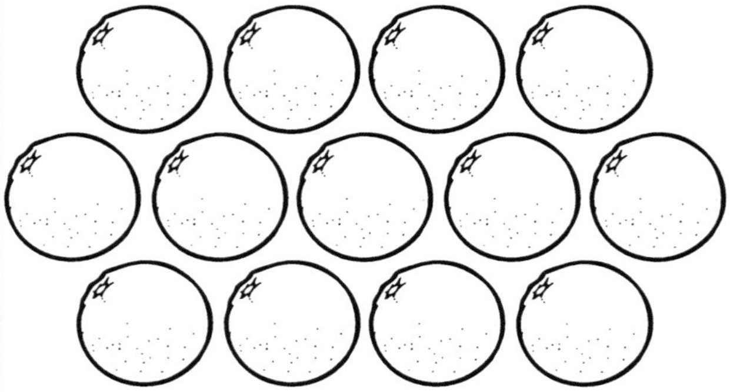

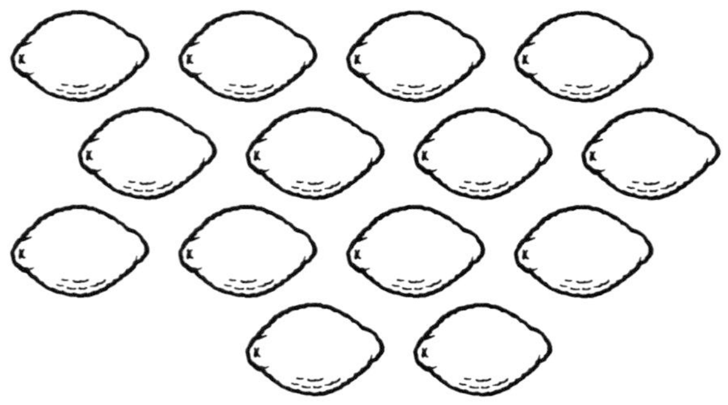

Name: _____

Writing Numbers 11-20

Teacher Directions: Have students count aloud the number of fruit in each row in the first column. Then, have students trace the numbers in the second column and, finally, write the number in the third column.

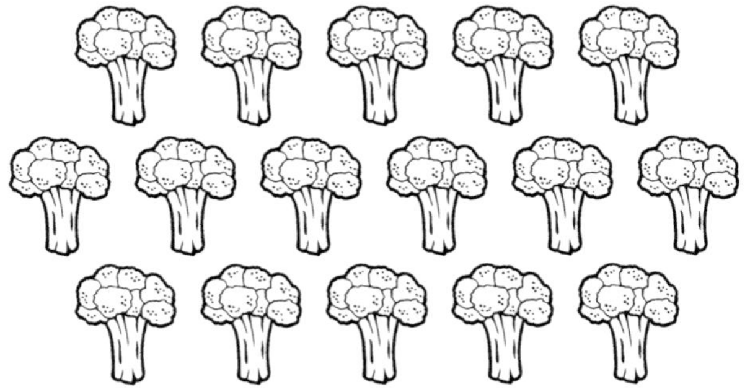

(broccoli)	16	
(pumpkins)	17	
(corn)	18	
(carrots)	19	

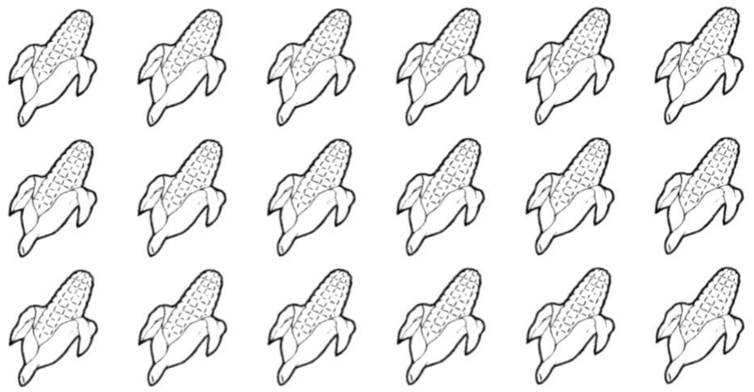

THINK & DRAW

Name: _____

Writing Numbers 11–20

Teacher Directions: Have students think about the numbers 11–20. Read the directions aloud to students.

Write the numbers 11–20 in order.

_____

- -

_____

- -

_____

_____

- -

_____

Draw 12 pieces of fruit in the box.

Name: _____

How Many? 1–10

Teacher Directions: Count from 1 to 10 aloud together as a class. Then, count aloud the objects for each number as a class. Ask students various questions, such as "How many stars do you see? How many moons are there?"

Let's learn about the numbers 1–10!

□	1	 ♡♡♡ ♡♡♡	6
✕ ✕	2	 ☆☆☆ ☆☆☆☆	7
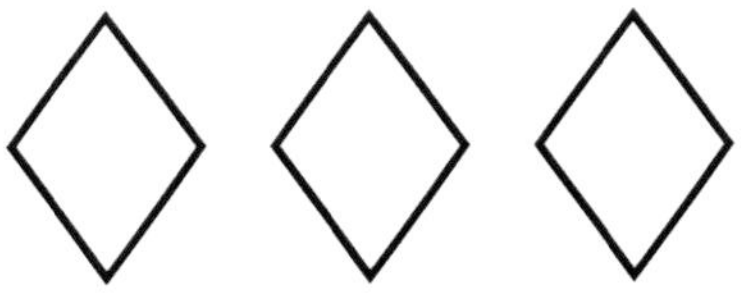 ◇◇◇	3	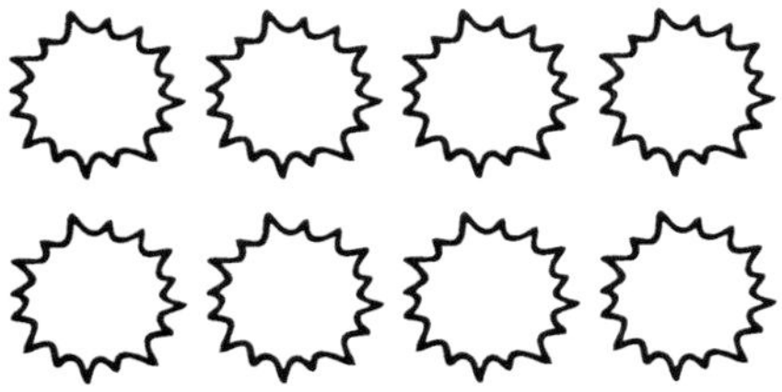 ✹✹✹✹ ✹✹✹✹	8
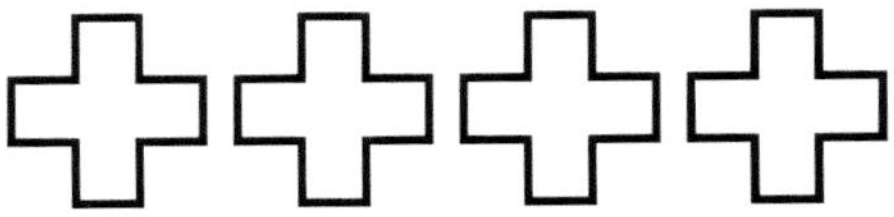 ✚✚✚✚	4	 △△△△ △△△△△	9
 ☾☾☾ ☾☾	5	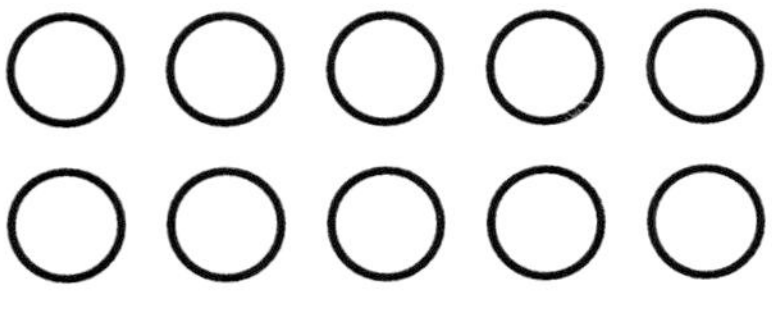 ○○○○○ ○○○○○	10

Name: _____

How Many? 1–10

Teacher Directions: Have students work with partners to count and color the correct number of objects to match the number.

2

9

6

8

Name: _____

How Many? 1–10

Teacher Directions: Have students count how many there are of each type of animal. Have them circle the correct numbers.

Teacher Directions: Have students count how many there are of each type of fruit. Have them write the correct number in the box.

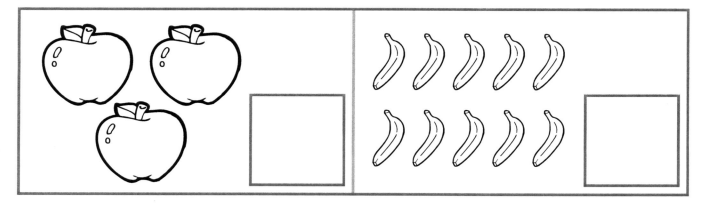

Teacher Directions: Have students color the correct number of faces.

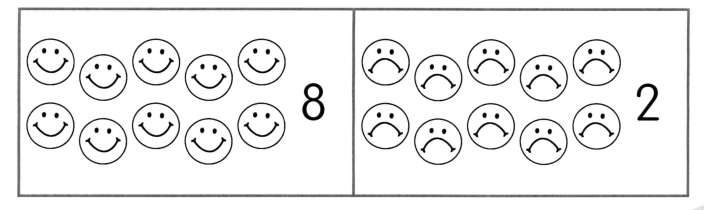

Name: _____

How Many? 1–10

Teacher Directions: Have students think about counting to 10. Read the directions aloud to students.

Count the people. How many are there?

Draw a picture that shows what you learned about counting to 10.

Counting & Cardinality

Name: _____

How Many? 11–20

Teacher Directions: Count from 11 to 20 aloud together as a class. Then, count aloud the objects for each number as a class. Ask students various questions, such as "How many stars do you see? How many moons are there?"

Let's learn about the numbers 11–20!

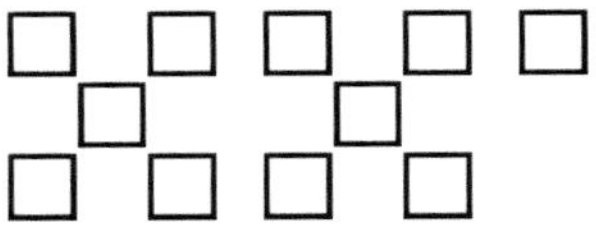 ▫▫▫▫▫▫▫▫▫	11	 ♡♡♡♡♡♡♡♡♡♡♡♡	16
 ✕✕✕✕✕✕✕✕✕✕✕✕	12	 ☆☆☆☆☆☆☆☆☆☆☆☆☆	17
 ◇◇◇◇◇◇◇◇◇◇◇◇	13	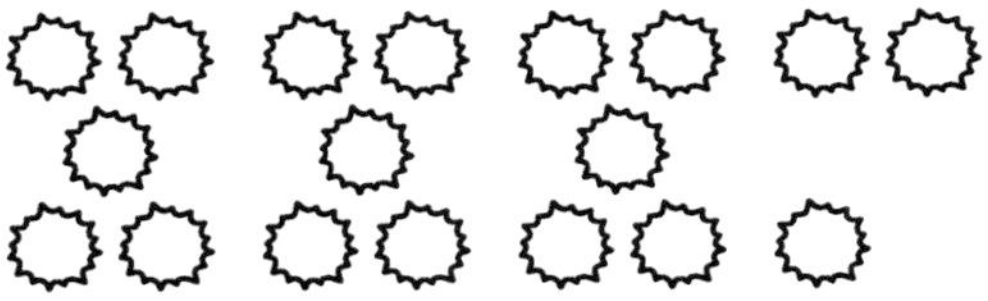 ✺✺✺✺✺✺✺✺✺✺✺✺✺✺	18
 ✚✚✚✚✚✚✚✚✚✚✚✚✚✚	14	 △△△△△△△△△△△△△△△	19
 ☾☾☾☾☾☾☾☾☾☾☾☾☾☾☾	15	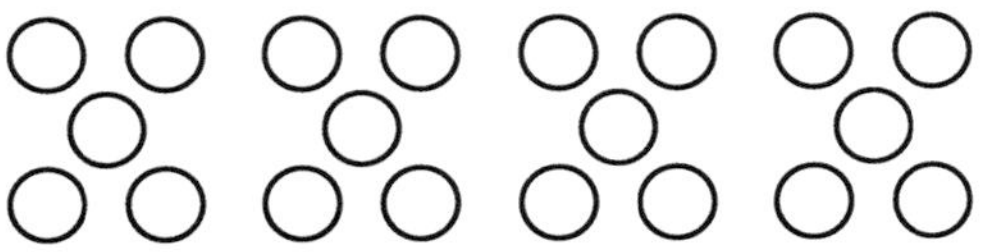 ○○○○○○○○○○○○○○○○	20

Name: _____

How Many? 11-20

Teacher Directions: Have students work with partners to count and color the correct number of objects to match the number.

11

17

13

19

Name: _____

How Many? 11-20

Teacher Directions: Have students count how many there are of each type of animal. Have them circle the correct numbers.

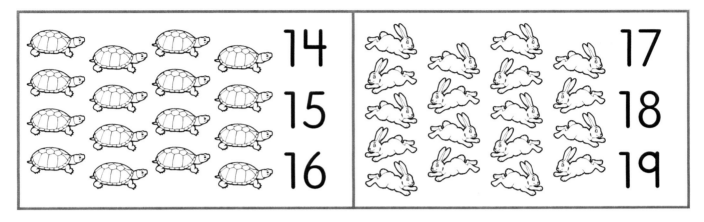

Teacher Directions: Have students count how many there are of each type of vegetable. Have them write the correct number in the box.

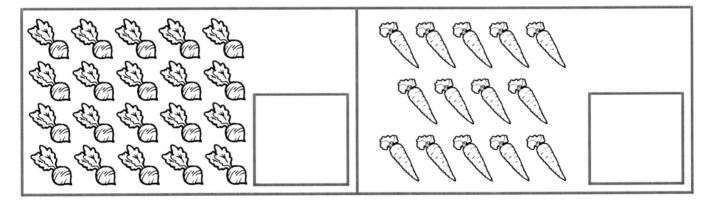

Teacher Directions: Have students color the correct number of desserts.

Name: _____

How Many? 11–20

Teacher Directions: Have students think about counting to 20. Read the directions aloud to students.

Count the bees. How many are there?

Draw a picture that shows what you learned about counting to 20.

#8292 Let's Get This Day Started: Math   ©*Teacher Created Resources*

LOOK & LEARN

More or Fewer

Teacher Directions: Tell students that we can compare numbers. Have students count the sets of animals aloud. Then, compare each set of numbers as a class. For example: 2 cows are more than 1, and 3 hens are fewer than 6.

cows

more

fewer

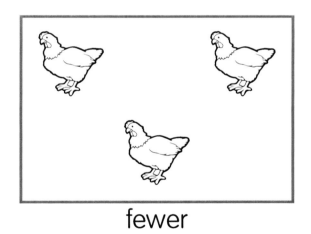

hens

fewer

more

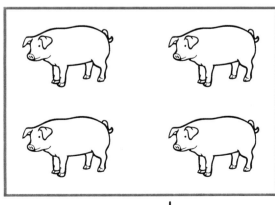

pigs

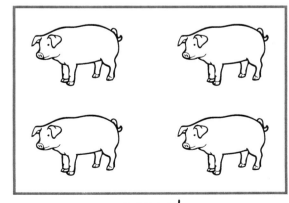

equal

equal

Name: _____

More or Fewer

Teacher Directions: Read the directions for each row aloud to students. Have students work with partners to color the correct answer. If time permits, have students write the number of animals in each scene.

Color the pond that has **more** ducks.

Color the mud puddle that has **fewer** pigs.

Color the fence that has **more** birds.

Name: _____

More or Fewer

Teacher Directions: Read aloud the directions for each row to students. Have students write the correct number in the box and color the correct answer.

Count the spots on each cow. Color the cow with **more** spots.

Count the spots on each horse. Color the horse with **fewer** spots.

Name: _____

More or Fewer

Teacher Directions: Have students think about comparing numbers. Read the directions aloud to students.

Color the nest with **more** chicks.

Draw a picture that shows what you learned about comparing numbers.

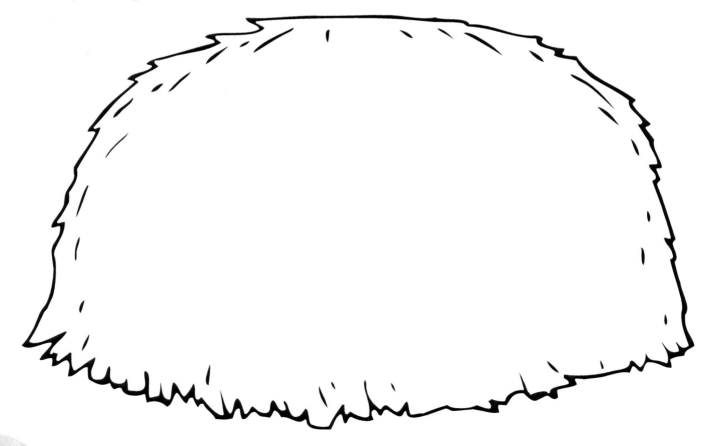

LOOK & LEARN

Name: _____

Comparing Numbers

Teacher Directions: Read the page aloud to students. Explain to students that the smallest number is 1. The numbers get bigger as they count up to 10. The numbers go from least to greatest.

Name: _____

Comparing Numbers

Teacher Directions: Have students work with partners to color the penguin that has the **greater** number in each set.

Teacher Directions: Have students work with partners to color the penguin that has the number that is **less** in each set.

Name: _____

Comparing Numbers

Teacher Directions: Have students color the polar bear that is sitting on the **greater** number in each set.

Teacher Directions: Have students color the polar bear that has the number that is **less** in each set.

Name: _____

Comparing Numbers

Teacher Directions: Have students think about comparing numbers. Read the directions and questions aloud to students.

Is the narwhal pointing to the bigger number or the smaller number? Circle the answer.

7   5

bigger / smaller

Draw a picture that shows what you learned about comparing numbers.

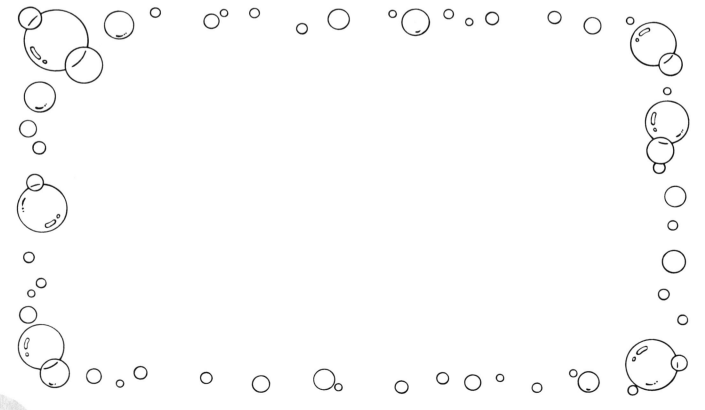

Name: _____

Counting with Ten Frames

Teacher Directions: Read the page aloud to students. Explain what a ten frame is. Have students count the empty spaces in the first ten frame with you. Ask students how many stars are in the second ten frame. How many are in the last ten frame?

This is a ten frame.

It helps us count.

5

10

PARTNER & PRACTICE

Name: _____

Counting with Ten Frames

Teacher Directions: Have students work with partners to count the number of stars in each ten frame. Have students write the correct number on the line.

_____

_____

_____

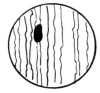  

#8292 Let's Get This Day Started: Math   ©*Teacher Created Resources*

Name: _____

Counting with Ten Frames

Teacher Directions: Have students draw the correct number of moons in the ten frame.

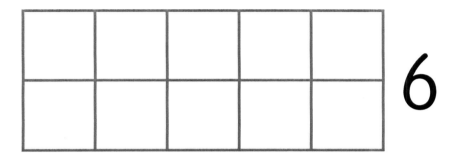

Teacher Directions: Have students write the number of moons shown in the ten frame.

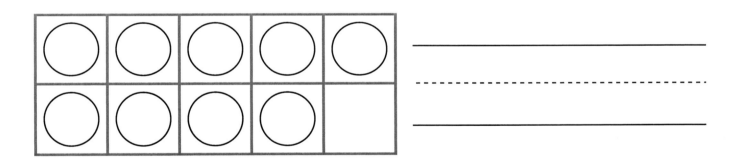

Teacher Directions: Have students fill in the ten frame with their favorite number and then write the number on the line.

THINK & DRAW

Name: _____

Counting with Ten Frames

Teacher Directions: Have students think about counting with ten frames. Read the directions and question aloud to students.

How many stars do you see?

☆	☆	☆	☆	☆
☆	☆	☆		

_____

- - - - - - - - - - - - - - - - - - -

_____

Draw a picture that shows what you learned about counting with ten frames.

       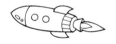   

Name: _____

Adding Objects

Teacher Directions: Read the page aloud to students. Explain that adding is putting two or more numbers or objects together to make a new total. Show students how to count all the objects together to get the answer.

Let's add!

How many bones does the dog have?

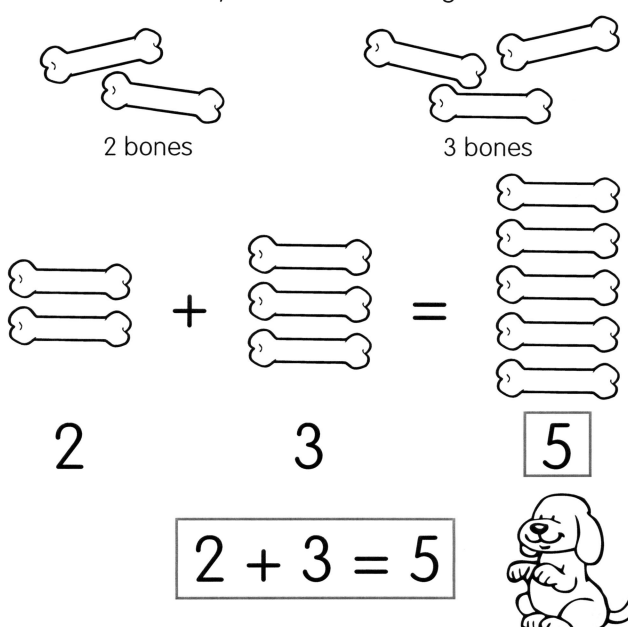

2 bones   3 bones

2   +   3   =   5

2 + 3 = 5

PARTNER & PRACTICE

Name: _____

Adding Objects

Teacher Directions: Have students work with partners to add together the objects and write the total number in the box.

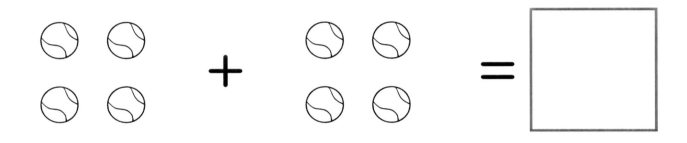

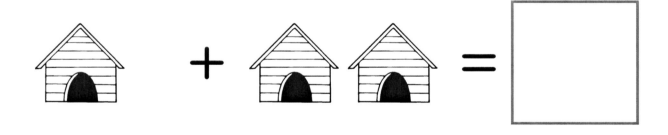

Adding & Subtracting

YOUR TURN

Adding Objects

Teacher Directions: Have students add together the dog faces and write the total number in the box.

©*Teacher Created Resources*   *#8292 Let's Get This Day Started: Math*   **35**

Name: _____

Adding Objects

Teacher Directions: Have students think about adding objects. Read the directions and questions aloud to students.

How many toys does this dog have?

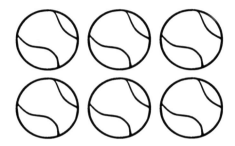 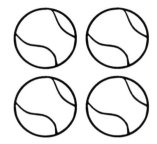

Draw a picture that shows what you learned about adding objects.

LOOK & LEARN

Name: _____

Subtracting Objects

Teacher Directions: Read the page aloud to students. Explain that subtracting is taking one number away from another. Show students how to count the remaining to get the answer.

Let's subtract!

The cat has 5 balls of yarn.

She gives 2 away.

How many does she have left?

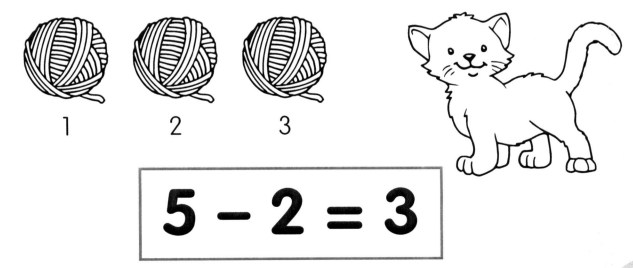

1   2   3

$$5 - 2 = 3$$

Name: _____

Subtracting Objects

Teacher Directions: Have students work with partners to subtract the objects and write the answer in the box.

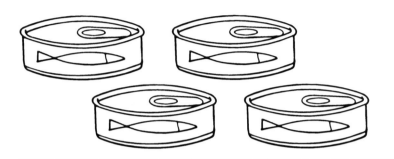

$4 - 3 =$ ☐

$10 - 5 =$ ☐

$7 - 1 =$ ☐

$8 - 4 =$ ☐

$6 - 2 =$ ☐

Name: _____

Subtracting Objects

Teacher Directions: Have students subtract the objects by crossing out the number of cats being subtracted and writing the answer in the box.

$5 - 1 =$

$5 - 4 =$

   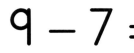

$9 - 7 =$

$2 - 2 =$

$10 - 8 =$

Name: _____

Subtracting Objects

Teacher Directions: Have students think about subtracting objects. Read the directions and question aloud to students.

The cat has 5 toys.

She lost 1 toy.

How many toys
are left?

Draw a picture that shows what you learned about subtracting objects.

Name: _____

Adding with Ten Frames

Teacher Directions: Read the page aloud to students. Remind students what a ten frame is. Explain how a ten frame can be a useful tool when adding two numbers together.

Ten frames help us add!

$$5 + 2 = ?$$

Count the shapes in the ten frame!

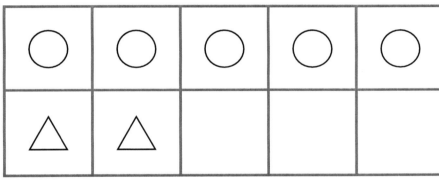

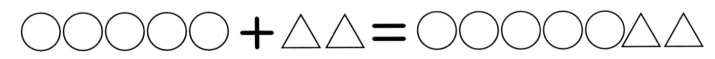

5   2   7

$$5 + 2 = 7$$

Name: _____

Adding with Ten Frames

Teacher Directions: Have students work with partners to draw shapes in the ten frames to help them find the answers. The first one has been done for them.

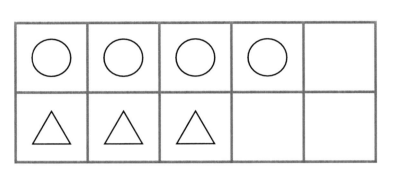

4 + 3 = 7

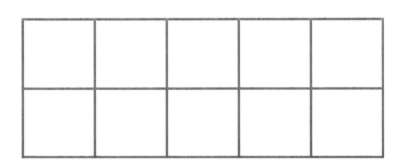

2 + 2 =

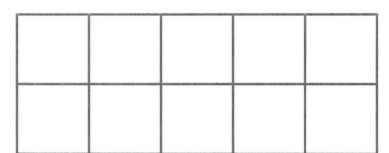

1 + 7 =

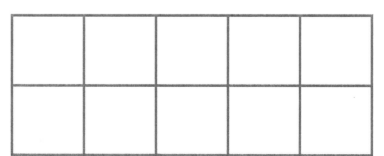

6 + 4 =

Name: _____

Adding with Ten Frames

Teacher Directions: Have students draw shapes in the ten frames to help them find the answers.

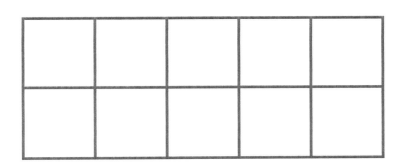

$5 + 5 =$

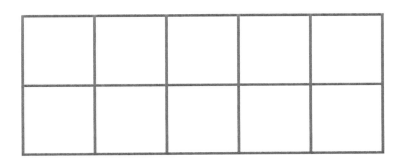

$8 + 1 =$

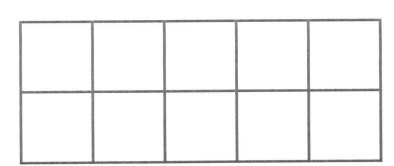

$4 + 2 =$

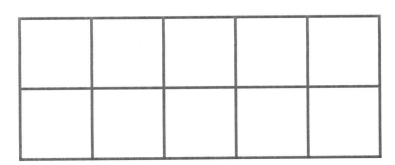

$3 + 5 =$

#8292 Let's Get This Day Started: Math

THINK & DRAW

Name: _____

Adding with Ten Frames

Teacher Directions: Have students think about adding with ten frames. Read the directions aloud to students.

Use the ten frame to find the answer. Write your answer in the box.

$3 + 3 = ?$

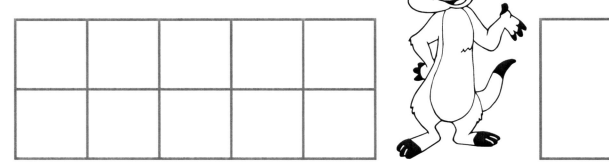

Draw a picture that shows what you learned about adding with ten frames.

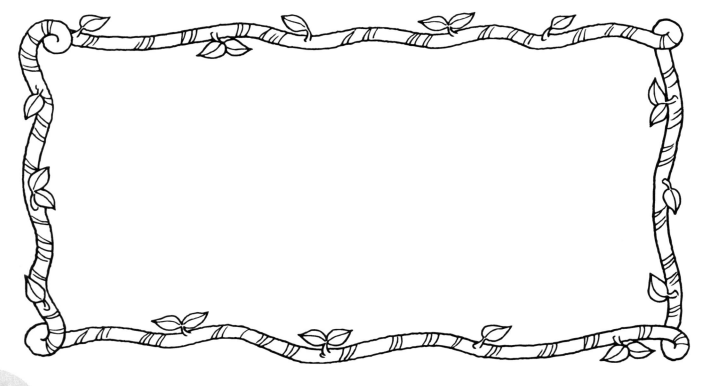

Name: _____

Subtracting with Ten Frames

Teacher Directions: Read the page aloud to students. Remind students what a ten frame is. Explain how a ten frame can be a useful tool when subtracting numbers.

Ten frames help us subtract!

$$5 - 2 = ?$$

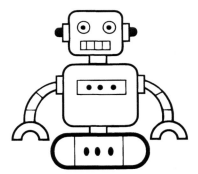

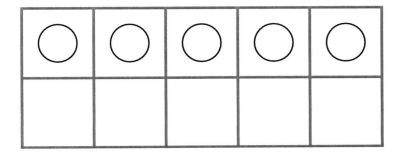

The first number tells us how many shapes to draw in our ten frame.

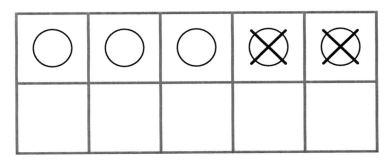

The second number tells us how many we subtract, or take away.

Count how many shapes are left.

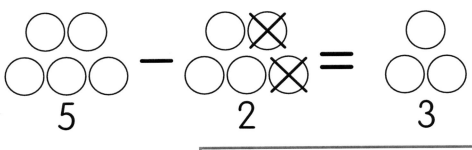

5   2   3

$$5 - 2 = 3$$

PARTNER & PRACTICE

Name: _____

Subtracting with Ten Frames

Teacher Directions: Have students work with partners to draw shapes in the ten frames and then cross out the correct number of shapes to help them find the answers. The first one has been done for them.

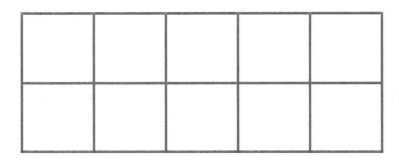

$4 - 3 = \boxed{1}$

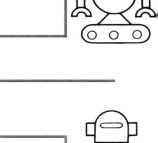

$8 - 6 = \boxed{}$

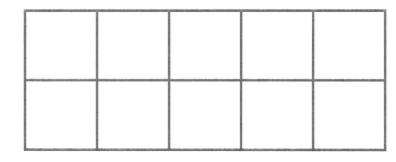

$7 - 5 = \boxed{}$

$2 - 2 = \boxed{}$

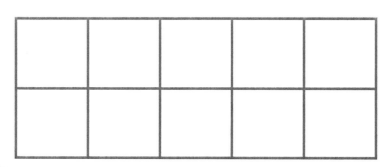

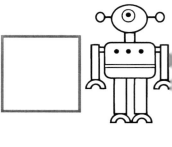

#8292 Let's Get This Day Started: Math

Name: _____

Subtracting with Ten Frames

Teacher Directions: Have students draw shapes in the ten frames and then cross out the correct number of shapes to help them find the answers.

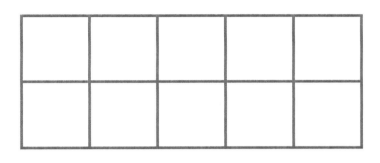

$3 - 1 = \boxed{}$

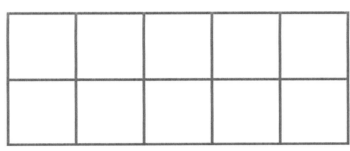

$9 - 4 = \boxed{}$

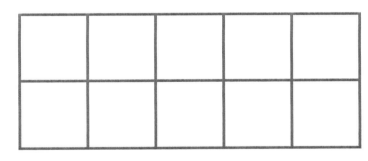

$6 - 2 = \boxed{}$

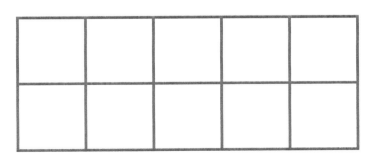

$10 - 5 = \boxed{}$

Name: _____

Subtracting with Ten Frames

Teacher Directions: Have students think about subtracting with ten frames. Read the directions aloud to students.

Use the ten frame to find the answer. Write your answer in the box.

$7 - 2 = ?$

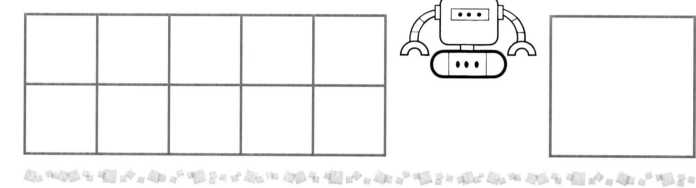

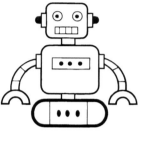

Draw a picture that shows what you learned about subtracting with ten frames.

LOOK & LEARN

Name: _____

Addition Equations

Teacher Directions: Read the page aloud to students. Talk about what an equation is. Discuss the different ways in which students know how to solve an addition equation.

This is an equation.

$$4 + 3 = \boxed{}$$

Let's solve it!

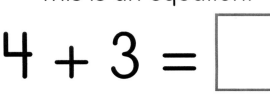

We can use…

mental math

4 + 3 = ?

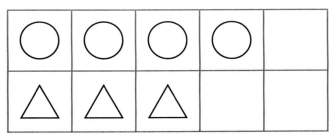

ten frames

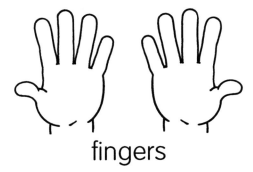

fingers

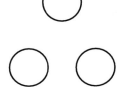

draw pictures

$$4 + 3 = 7$$

Adding & Subtracting

Name: _____

Addition Equations

Teacher Directions: Have students work with partners to solve the addition equations. The first one has been done for them.

$$2 + 2 = 4$$

$$5 + 2 = \boxed{}$$

$$3 + 6 = \boxed{}$$

$$7 + 1 = \boxed{}$$

$$4 + 5 = \boxed{}$$

#8292 Let's Get This Day Started: Math ©*Teacher Created Resources*

Addition Equations

Teacher Directions: Have students solve the addition equations and color the dinosaur, using the correct colors. Help students color the key at the bottom first to ensure that they use the proper colors for each number.

$1 + 1 = \boxed{}$ $2 + 4 = \boxed{}$

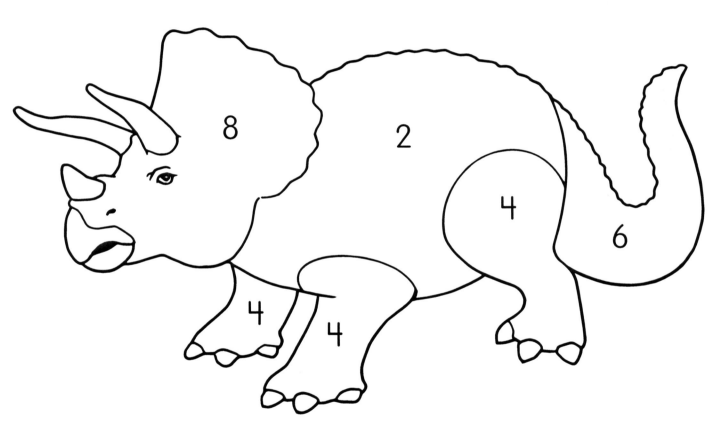

$3 + 1 = \boxed{}$ $6 + 2 = \boxed{}$

| 2 = green | 4 = purple | 6 = orange | 8 = yellow |

THINK & DRAW

Name: _____

Addition Equations

Teacher Directions: Have students think about solving addition equations. Read the directions aloud to students.

Write an equation for this picture.

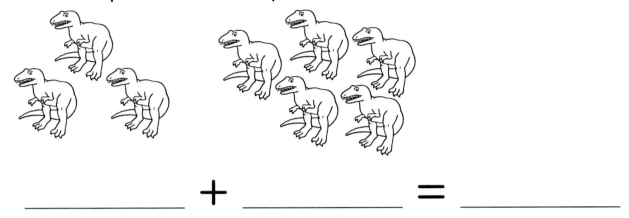

_____ **+** _____ **=** _____

Draw a picture that shows what you learned about solving addition equations.

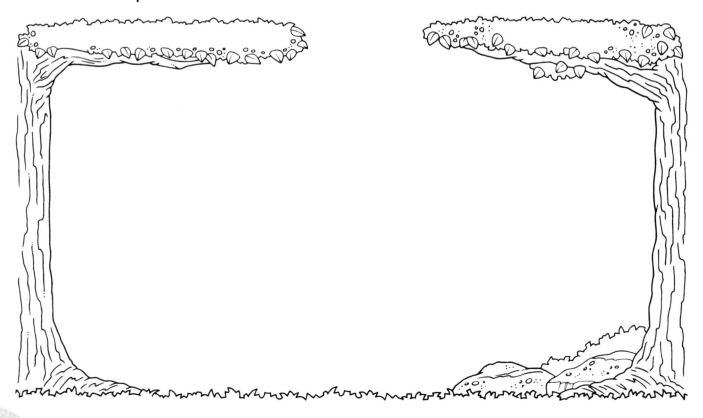

Adding & Subtracting

Name: _____

Subtraction Equations

Teacher Directions: Read the page aloud to students. Remind students what an equation is. Discuss the different ways in which students know how to solve a subtraction equation.

This is an equation.

$$4 - 3 = \boxed{}$$

Let's solve it!

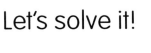

$4 - 3 = ?$

We can use...

mental math

ten frames

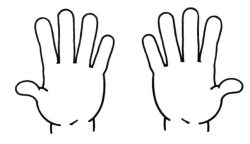

fingers

draw pictures

$$4 - 3 = 1$$

Name: _____

Subtraction Equations

Teacher Directions: Have students work with partners to solve the subtraction equations. The first one has been done for them.

$4 - 2 = \boxed{2}$

$7 - 3 = \boxed{}$

$9 - 8 = \boxed{}$

$3 - 2 = \boxed{}$

$10 - 1 = \boxed{}$

#8292 Let's Get This Day Started: Math

Name: _____

Subtraction Equations

Teacher Directions: Have students solve the subtraction equations and color the flower, using the correct colors. Help students color the key at the bottom first to ensure that they use the proper colors for each number.

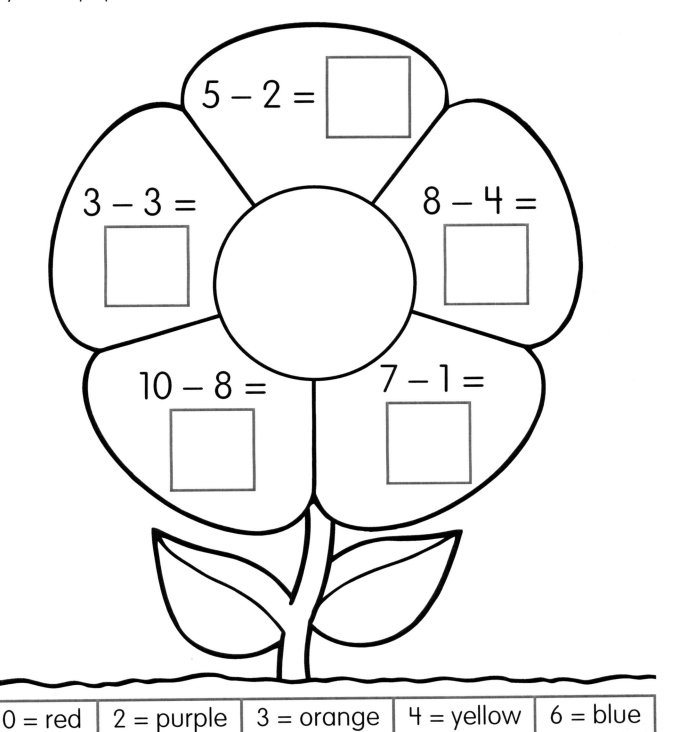

0 = red	2 = purple	3 = orange	4 = yellow	6 = blue

Name: _____

Subtraction Equations

Teacher Directions: Have students think about solving subtraction equations. Read the directions aloud to students.

Write an equation for this picture.

_____ **−** _____ **=** _____

Draw a picture that shows what you learned about solving subtraction equations.

Name: _____

Making 10

Teacher Directions: Read the page aloud to students. Talk about how each number 0–10 can be added to another number (0–10) to make 10. Discuss the different ways to make 10.

When put together, these numbers make 10.

10	0
9	1
8	2
7	3
6	4
5	5
4	6
3	7
2	8
1	9
0	10

Let's look at 6 and 4.

Together, they make 10!

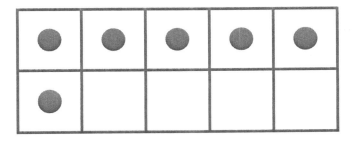

6   +   4   =   10

There are 4 empty boxes.

This tells us 6 and 4 make 10.

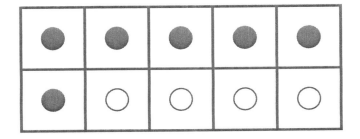

$$6 + 4 = 10$$

Name: _____

Making 10

Teacher Directions: Have students color each band of the rainbow a different color. Students will need 7 different colors. When students are finished coloring, have them work with partners and use the rainbow to help them find the missing numbers in the equations.

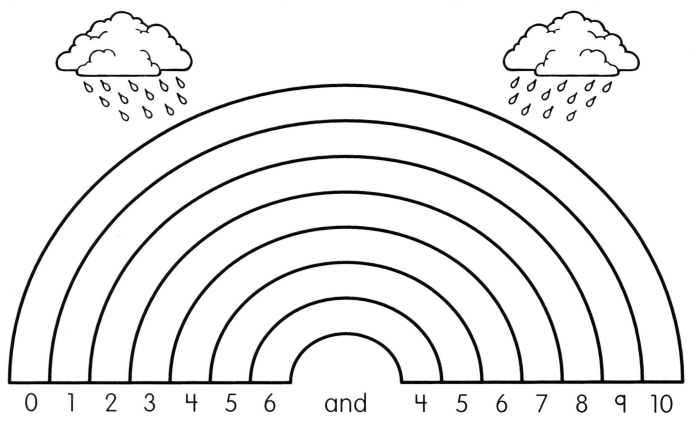

$$2 + \boxed{} = 10$$

$$4 + \boxed{} = 10$$

$$6 + \boxed{} = 10$$

$$\boxed{} + 10 = 10$$

$$\boxed{} + 7 = 10$$

$$\boxed{} + 5 = 10$$

#8292 Let's Get This Day Started: Math ©*Teacher Created Resources*

Name: _____

Making 10

Teacher Directions: Have students use the ten frames to help them find the missing numbers in the equations.

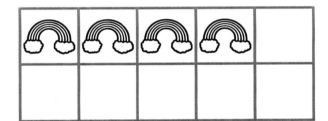

$7 + \boxed{} = 10$

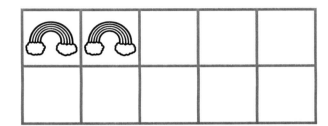

$2 + \boxed{} = 10$

$\boxed{} + 4 = 10$

$\boxed{} + 1 = 10$

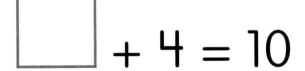

$5 + \boxed{} = 10$

$3 + \boxed{} = 10$

THINK & DRAW

Name: _____

Making 10

Teacher Directions: Have students think about making 10. Read the directions and questions aloud to students.

Count the clouds. How many more do you need to make 10?

Draw a picture in the cloud that shows what you learned about making 10.

#8292 Let's Get This Day Started: Math ©*Teacher Created Resources*

Name: _____

Ten and Some Ones

Teacher Directions: Count aloud to 20 with students. Read the page aloud to students. Talk about how numbers 11–19 are composed of 10 and some ones.

11

12

13

14

15

16

17

18

19

Count the flies.

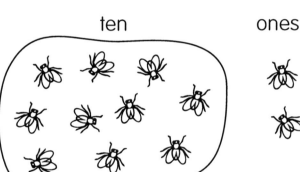

There are 12.

We can make a group of 10 and some ones.

ten   ones

10 + 2 = 12

Here are more ways we can look at the number 12.

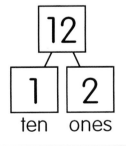

12

1   2
ten   ones

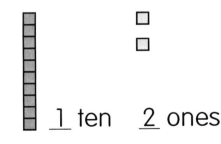

_1_ ten   _2_ ones

10   2

Name: _____

Ten and Some Ones

Teacher Directions: Have students work with partners to find the tens and ones.

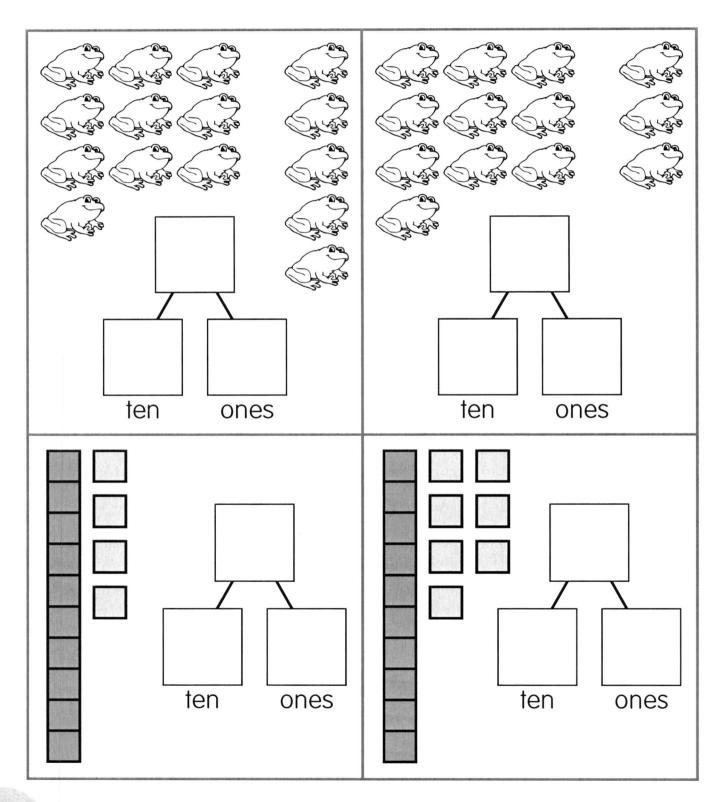

Name: _____

Ten and Some Ones

Teacher Directions: Have students find the tens and ones. The first one has been done for them.

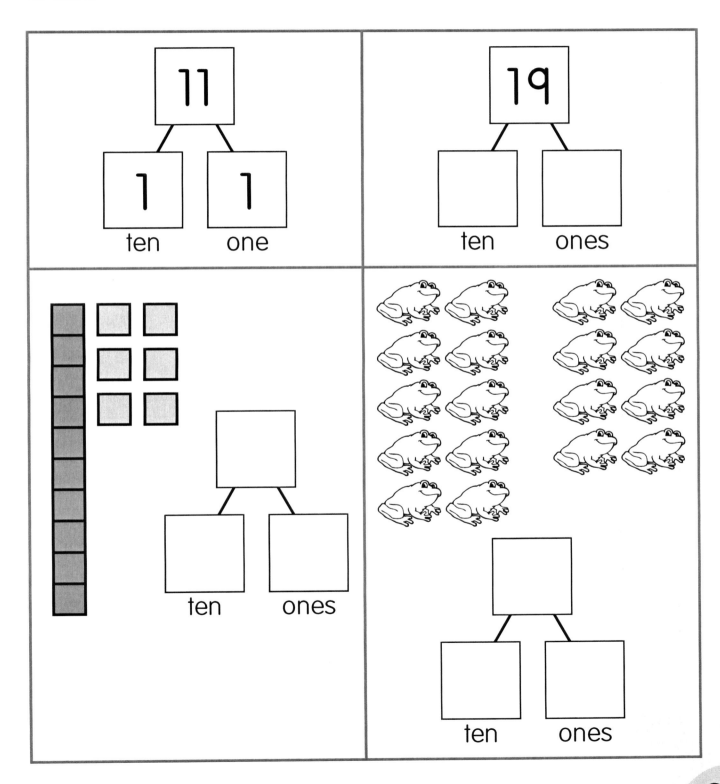

Ten and Some Ones

Teacher Directions: Have students think about the numbers 11–19 and how they are made of ten and some ones. Read the directions and questions aloud to students.

Name: _____

How many tens and ones are in the number 18?

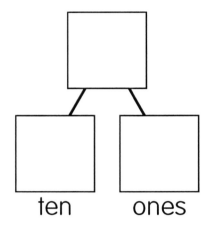

ten   ones

Draw a picture in the pond that shows what you learned about tens and ones.

Name: _____

Bigger, Smaller

Teacher Directions: Read the page aloud to students. Talk about comparing objects by using the words *bigger* and *smaller*.

These bears are different sizes.

This bear is **small**.

This bear is **big**.

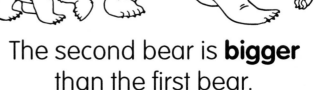

The first bear is **smaller** than the second bear.

The second bear is **bigger** than the first bear.

Name: _____

Bigger, Smaller

Teacher Directions: Have students work with partners to circle the **bigger** animal.

Which is bigger?

Teacher Directions: Have students work with partners to circle the **smaller** animal.

Which is smaller?

Name: _____

Bigger, Smaller

Teacher Directions: Have students circle the **smaller** animal.

Which is smaller?

Teacher Directions: Have students circle the **bigger** animal.

Which is bigger?

Name: _____

Bigger, Smaller

Teacher Directions: Have students think about comparing sizes using the words *bigger* and *smaller*. Read the directions and questions aloud to students.

Which is bigger, the bear or the squirrel?

Draw a picture that shows what you learned about comparing sizes.

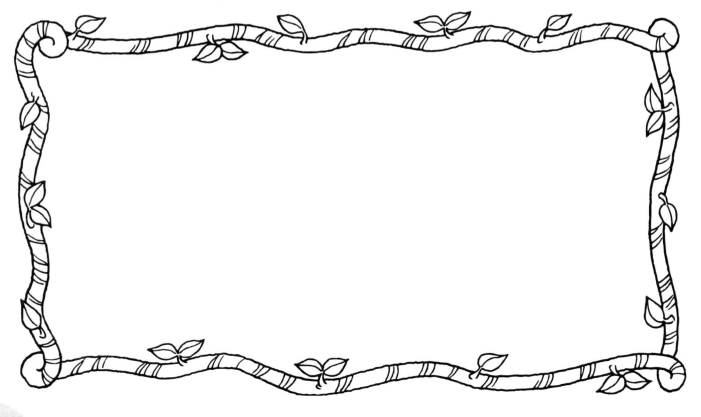

Name: _____

Longer, Shorter

Teacher Directions: Read the page aloud to students. Talk about comparing objects by using the words *longer* and *shorter*.

These pencils are different sizes.

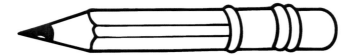

This pencil is **short**.

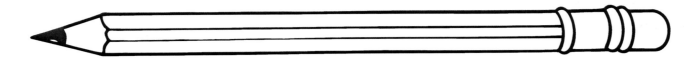

This pencil is **long**.

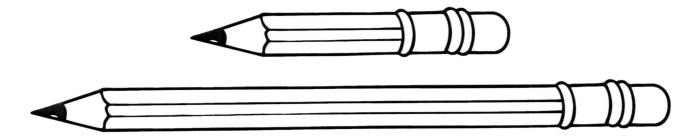

The top pencil is **shorter** than the bottom pencil.

The bottom pencil is **longer** than the top pencil.

Measurement

Name: _____

Longer, Shorter

Teacher Directions: Have students work with partners to check the box next to the **shorter** object.

Which is shorter?

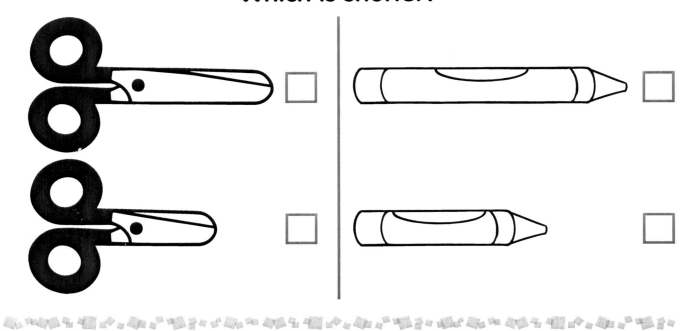

Teacher Directions: Have students work with partners to check the box next to the **longer** object.

Which is longer?

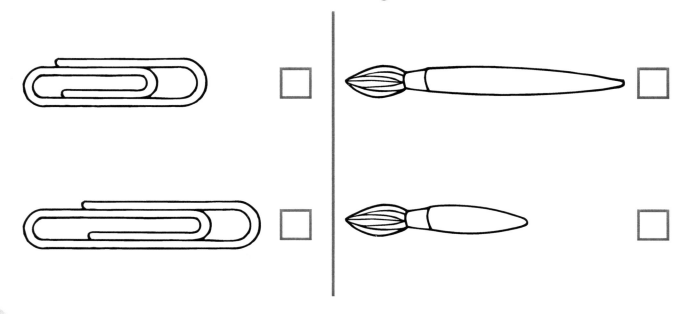

Name: _____

Longer, Shorter

Teacher Directions: Have students check the box next to the **longer** object.

Which is longer?

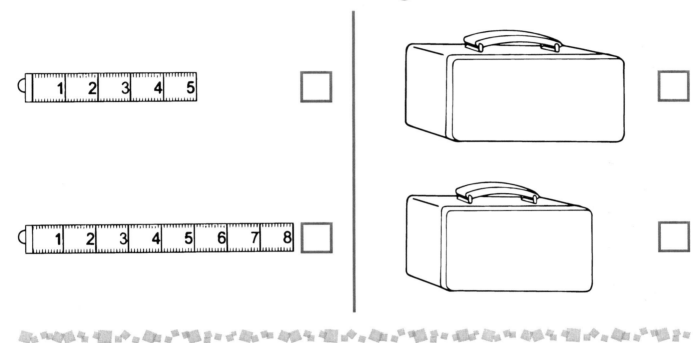

Teacher Directions: Have students check the box next to the **shorter** object.

Which is shorter?

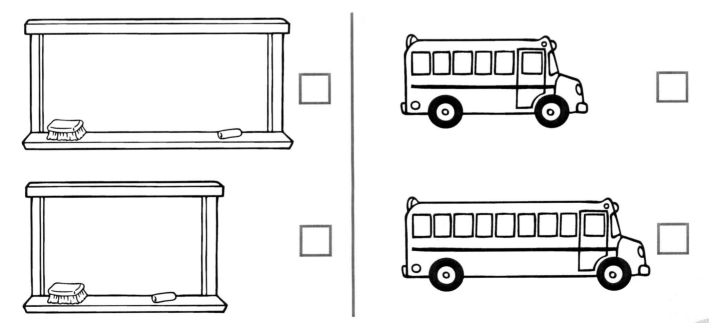

Name: _____

Longer, Shorter

Teacher Directions: Have students think about comparing things using the words *longer* and *shorter*. Read the directions aloud to students.

Draw a pencil longer than this one.

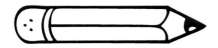

Draw a picture that shows what you learned about comparing lengths.

Name: _____

Heavier, Lighter

Teacher Directions: Read the page aloud to students. Talk about comparing the weight of different objects.

An elephant is **heavy**.

An elephant is **heavier** than a mouse.

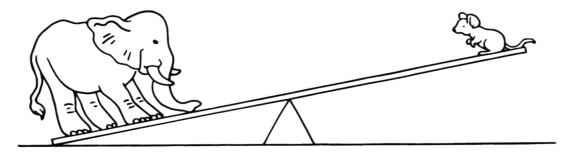

A feather is **light**.

A feather is **lighter** than a clown.

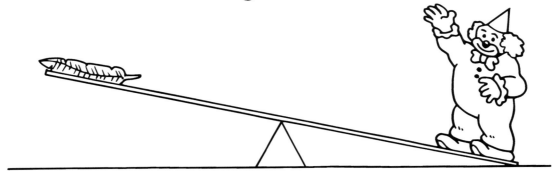

Name: _____

Heavier, Lighter

Teacher Directions: Have students work with partners to circle the **heavier** object.

Which is heavier?

Teacher Directions: Have students work with partners to circle the **lighter** object.

Which is lighter?

Name: _____

Heavier, Lighter

Teacher Directions: Have students cut out the objects at the bottom of the page and paste them in the correct column.

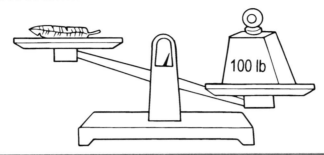

Light	Heavy

#8292 Let's Get This Day Started: Math **75**

Name: _____

Heavier, Lighter

Teacher Directions: Have students think about comparing things using the words *heavier* and *lighter*. Read the directions aloud to students.

Draw something that is lighter than an elephant.

Draw a picture that shows what you learned about comparing things that are heavy and light.

☆ ☆ ☆ ☆ ☆ ☆ ☆ ☆ ☆ ☆ ☆ ☆ ☆ ☆ ☆

☆ ☆

Name: _____

More or Less

Teacher Directions: Read the page aloud to students. Talk about comparing things using the words *more* and *less*.

Which ice cream has more scoops?

more scoops

less scoops

less sprinkles

more sprinkles

Name: _____

More or Less

Teacher Directions: Have students work with partners to compare the trays of candies and the trays of doughnuts. Have them write *more* or *less* under each tray.

_____

- - - - - - - - - - - - - - - - - -

_____

_____

- - - - - - - - - - - - - - - - - -

_____

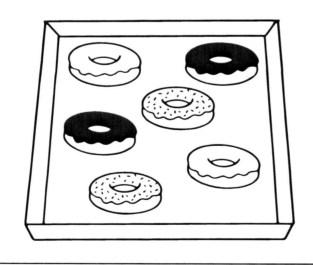

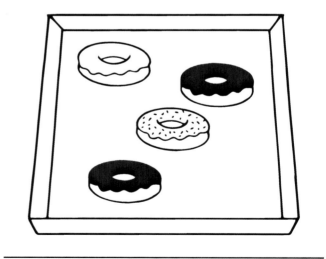

_____

- - - - - - - - - - - - - - - - - -

_____

_____

- - - - - - - - - - - - - - - - - -

_____

Name: _____

More or Less

Teacher Directions: Have students count the number of chocolate chips in each cookie and then color the cookie in each row with **more** chips.

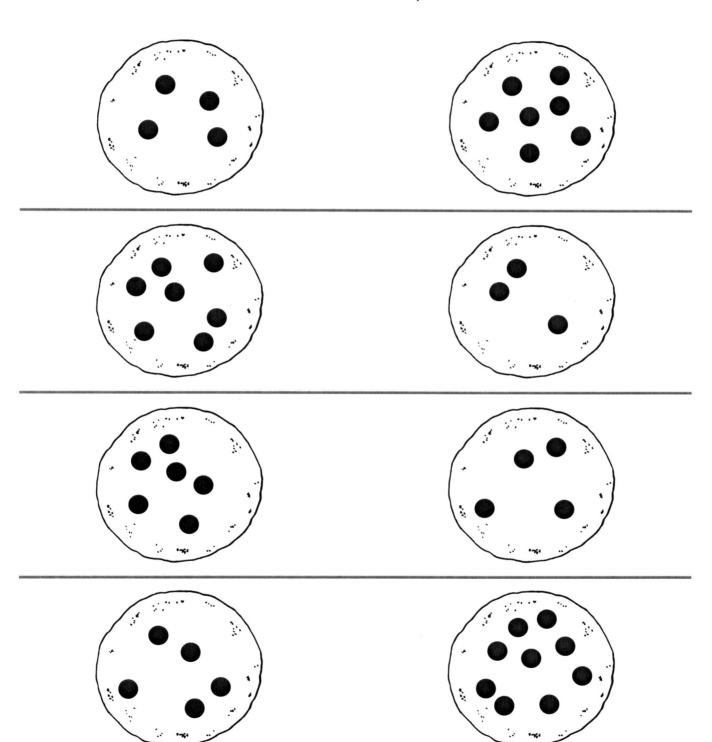

Name: _____

More or Less

Teacher Directions: Have students think about comparing objects using the words *more* and *less*. Read the directions aloud to students.

Draw an ice cream cone that has more scoops than this one.

Draw a picture that shows what you learned about the words *more* and *less*.

Name: _____

Sorting

Teacher Directions: Read the page aloud to students. Talk about classifying or sorting objects into categories or groups. Ask what objects they see. Then, work as a class to find 7 jewels, 4 necklaces, 2 crowns, and 1 sword in the pile of treasure below.

Let's sort the treasure.

How many jewels do you see?

How many necklaces do you see?

How many crowns do you see?

How many swords do you see?

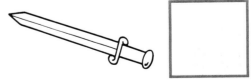

Name: _____

Sorting

Teacher Directions: Have students work with partners to sort the marine life swimming around the pirate ship. Have them color the sharks blue, the fish yellow, and the octopuses orange. Then, have them count how many there are of each and write the correct number in the box.

Name: _____

Sorting

Teacher Directions: Have students help the pirate sort out what he found. Which is treasure and which is trash? Cut out each object, and paste it in the right place.

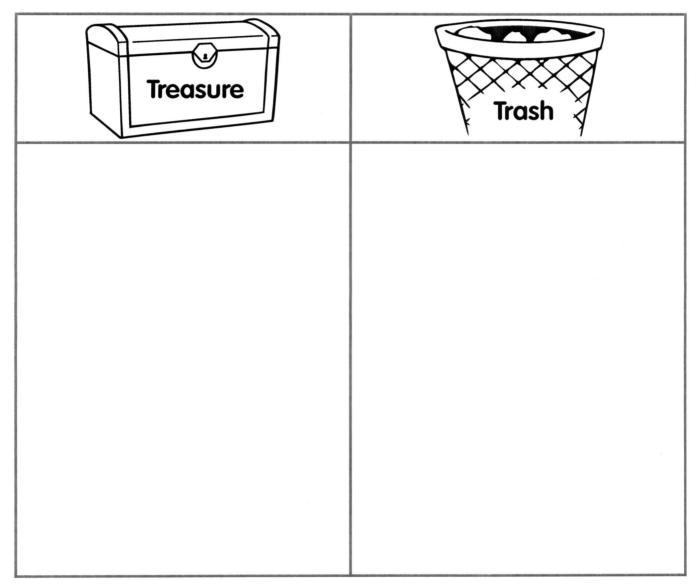

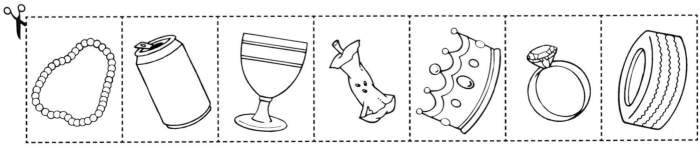

Measurement

Measurement

Measurement

Measurement

Name: _____

Sorting

Teacher Directions: Have students think about sorting objects. Read the directions and questions aloud to students.

How many jewels do you see? 　　How many necklaces are there?

  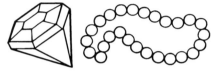 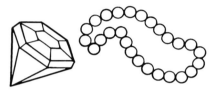

Draw a picture that shows what you learned about sorting objects.

Name: _____

Graphing

Teacher Directions: Read the page aloud to students. Talk about picture graphs. Explain that graphs help us sort information. Tell students that picture graphs give us information without using words. As a class, graph the birds students see in the picture. Count the number of each type of bird. Have students color in the squares on the graph accordingly.

	1	2	3	4	5

Name: _____

Graphing

Teacher Directions: Have students work with partners to cut out the squares at the bottom of the page and place them in the correct spots on the graph. When students have finished, ask the class some questions about the graph, such as "How many birds are there? Were there more birdhouses or bird feeders?"

Name: _____

Graphing

Teacher Directions: Have students color the chickens red, the owls blue, and the penguins yellow. Then, have them count each type of bird and color the squares on the graph accordingly.

Name: _____

Graphing

Teacher Directions: Have students think about comparing picture graphs. Read the directions and questions aloud to students.

Look at the picture. Look at the graph. What is missing from the graph? Fix the graph.

Draw a picture that shows what you learned about picture graphs.

Name: _____

Naming Shapes

Teacher Directions: Read the page aloud to students. Talk about the names of shapes. Explain that a shape keeps its name even if it is small, big, upside down, or sideways.

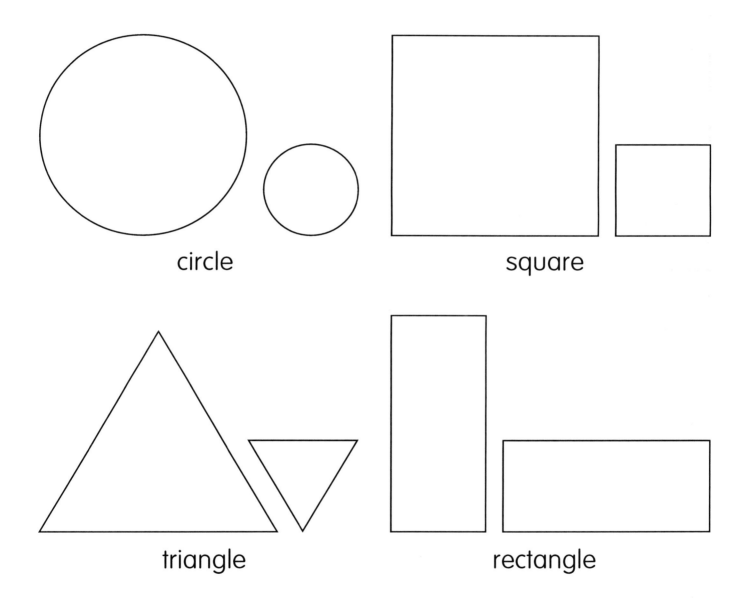

circle   square

triangle   rectangle

Name: _____

Naming Shapes

Teacher Directions: Have students work with partners to color all the shapes that match the labeled shape in each row.

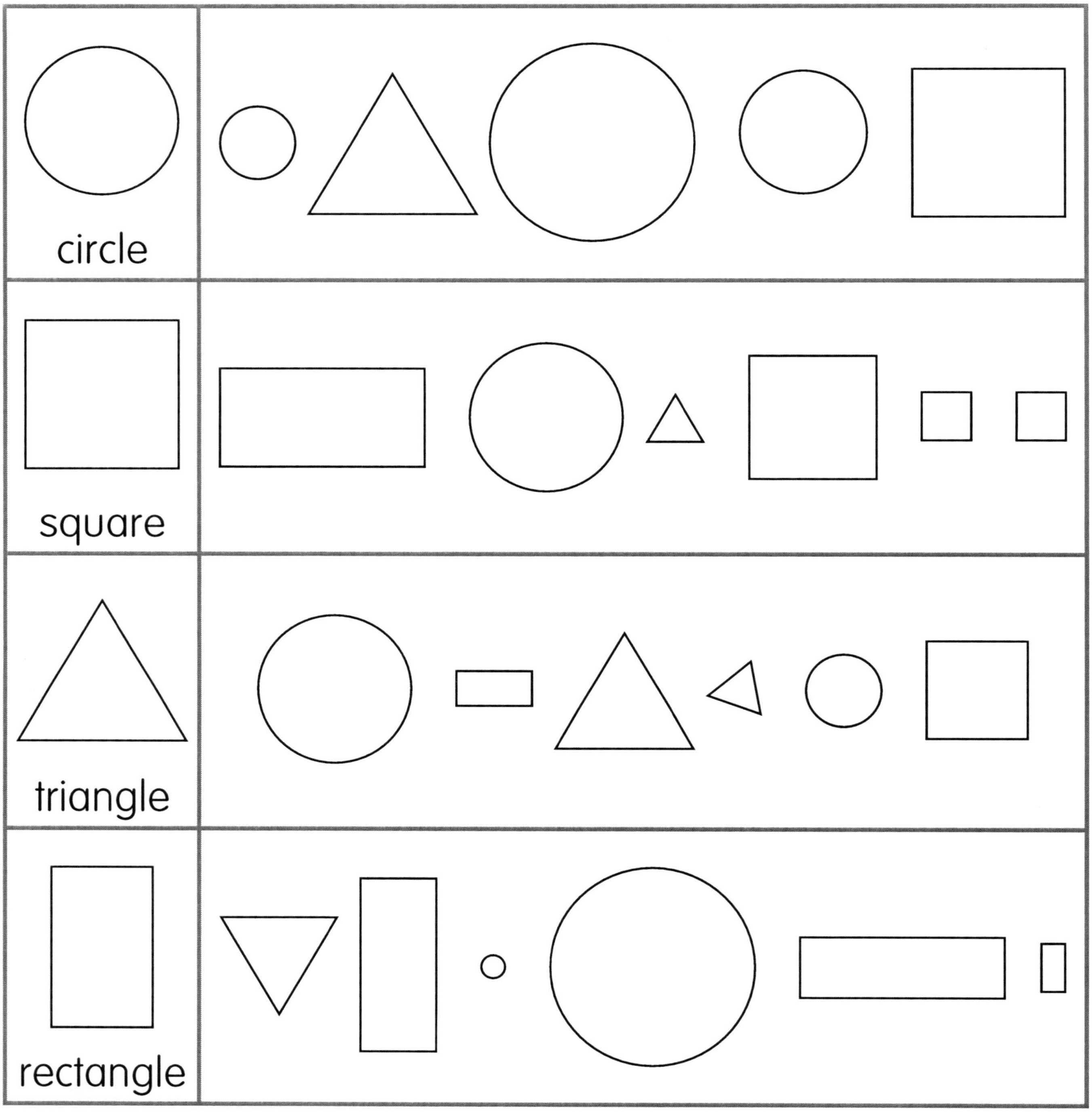

circle

square

triangle

rectangle

Name: _____

Naming Shapes

Teacher Directions: Have students color the shapes in the picture, using the colors in the key. Help students color the key first to ensure they use the proper colors for each shape.

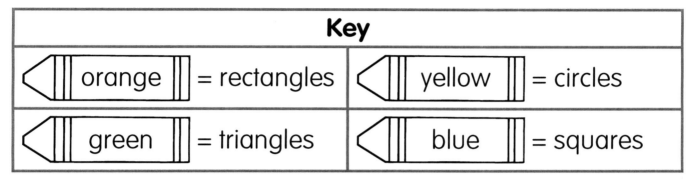

Key		
orange = rectangles	yellow = circles
green = triangles	blue = squares

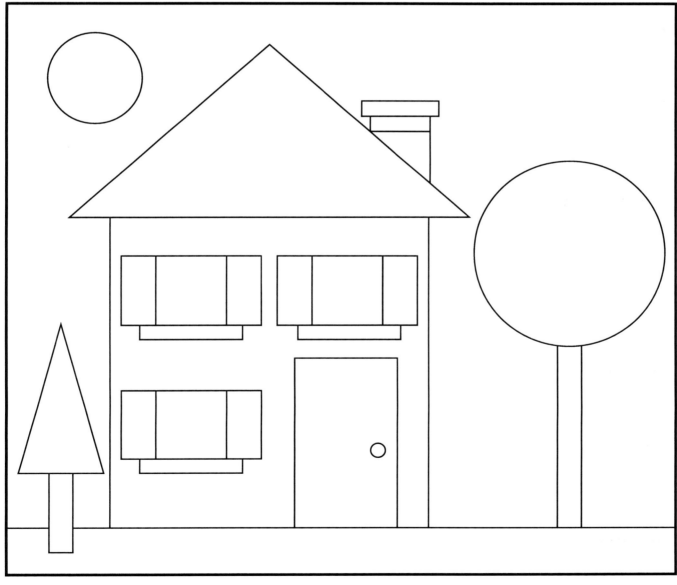

THINK &
DRAW

Name: _____

Naming Shapes

Teacher Directions: Have students think about naming shapes. Read the directions aloud to students.

Color all the triangles you see below.

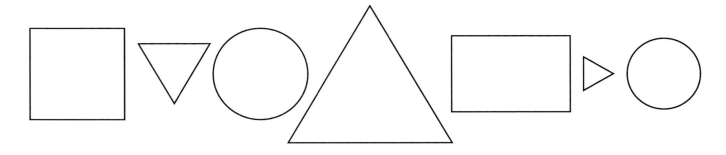

Draw a picture that shows what you learned about naming shapes.

#8292 Let's Get This Day Started: Math ©*Teacher Created Resources*

Name: _____

Where's the Shape?

Teacher Directions: Read the page aloud to students. Talk about how we can describe objects in our environment by using the following words and phrases: *above*, *below*, *behind*, *in front of*, and *next to*.

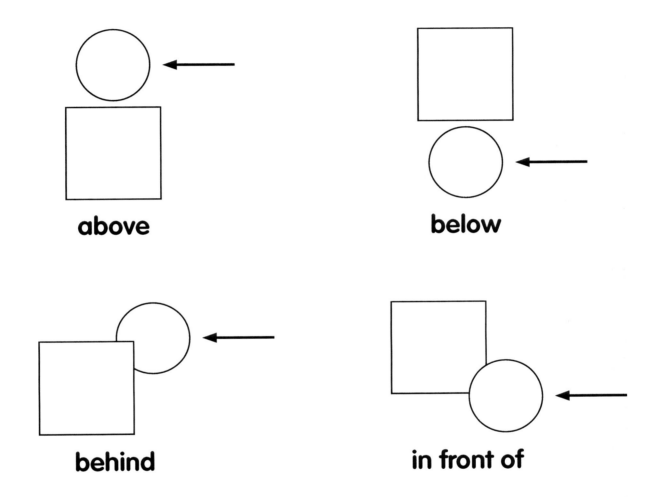

above　　　　　　　**below**

behind　　　　　　　**in front of**

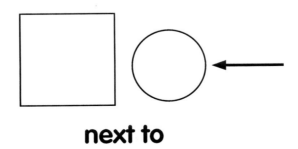

next to

Name: _____

Where's the Shape?

Teacher Directions: Have students work with partners to circle the pair of shapes that match each sentence. Read the sentences aloud to the class.

The circle is **behind** the square.

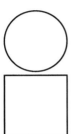      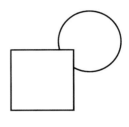

The triangle is **next to** the rectangle.

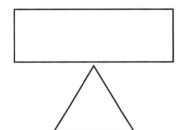   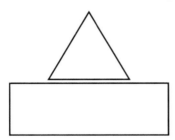   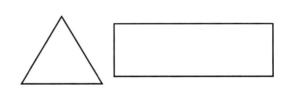

The square is **above** the triangle.

   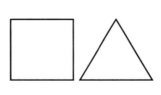   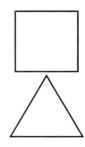

The rectangle is **in front of** the circle.

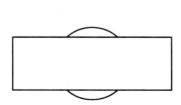   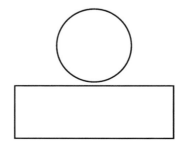   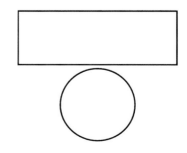

Name: _____

Where's the Shape?

Teacher Directions: Read each sentence aloud. Have students draw the correct shape in the correct spot.

Draw a circle **next to** the dog.

Draw a circle **above** the dog.

Draw a circle **below** the dog.

Draw a circle **in front of** the dog.

Name: _____

Where's the Shape?

Teacher Directions: Have students think about the words *above, below, behind, in front of,* and *next to.* Read the directions aloud to students.

Finish this scene by following the directions.

Draw a sun above the doghouse.

Draw a ball next to the doghouse.

Draw a picture that shows what you learned about describing the location of shapes.

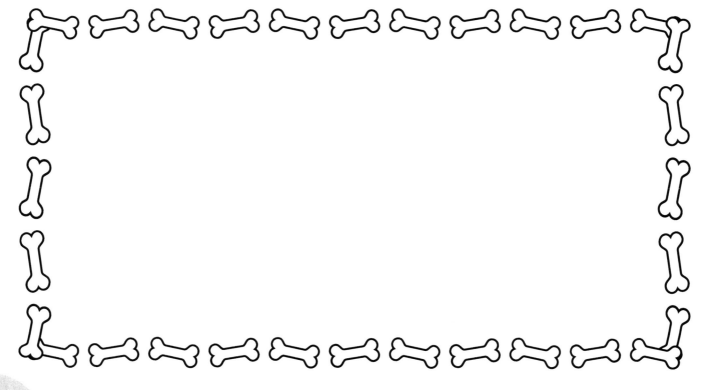

Name: _____

Shapes in Our World

Teacher Directions: Read the page aloud to students. Talk about how shapes are all around us.

When you look around, what shapes do you see?

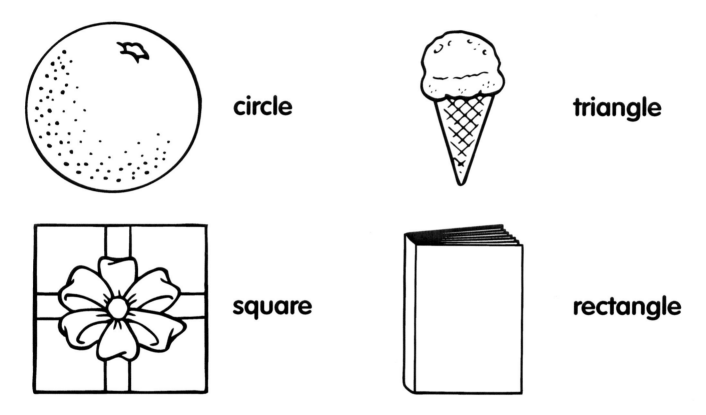

circle

triangle

square

rectangle

Everything is made up of shapes.

SCHOOL BUS

Name: _____

Shapes in Our World

Teacher Directions: Have students work with partners to find the shape in each row that does not match and cross it out.

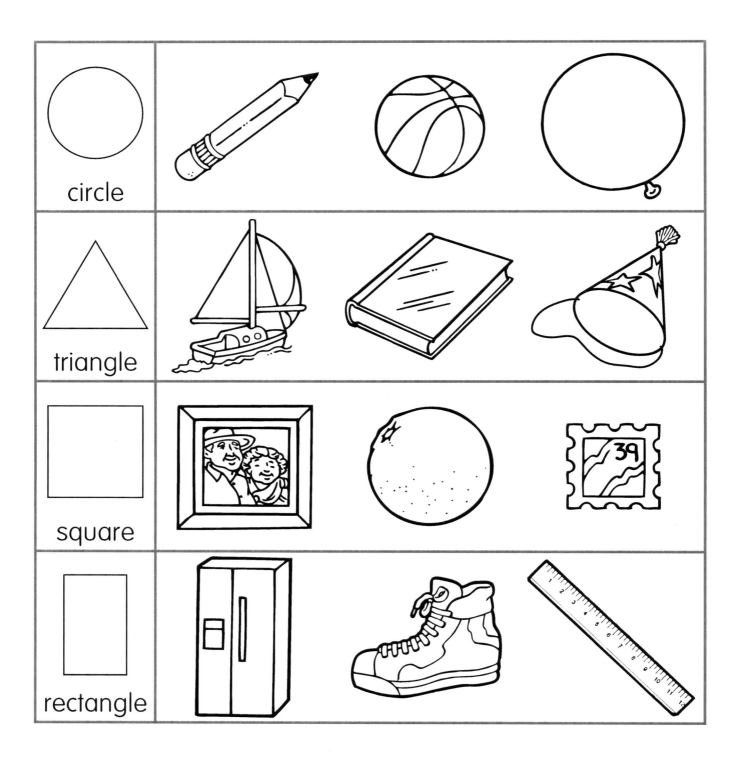

#8292 Let's Get This Day Started: Math   ©*Teacher Created Resources*

Name: _____

Shapes in Our World

Teacher Directions: Have students use the key below to color the shapes they find in the picture. Help students color the key first to ensure they use the proper colors for each shape.

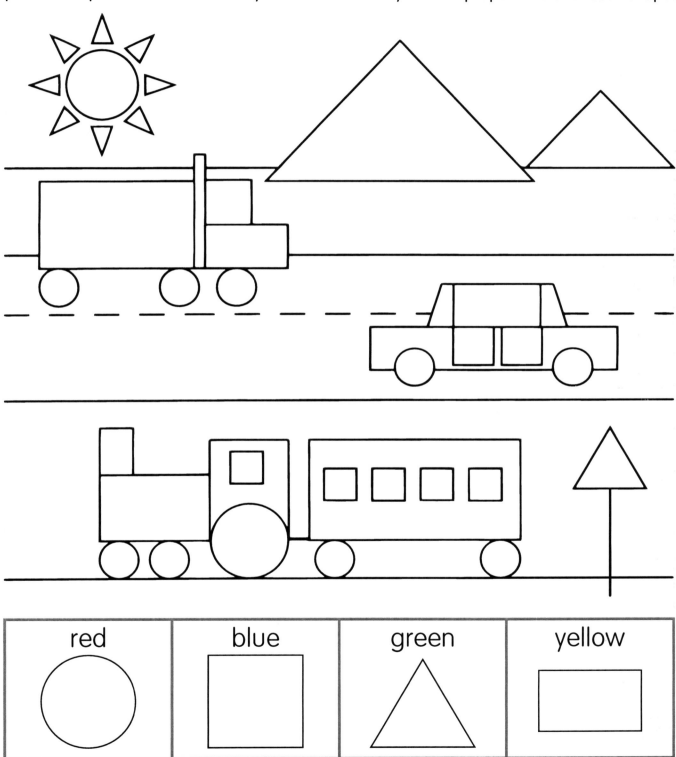

red	blue	green	yellow

Name: _____

Shapes in Our World

Teacher Directions: Have students think about all the different shapes they see in the world. Read the directions aloud to students.

Make an ice cream cone using shapes.

Draw a picture that shows the different shapes you saw in the world today.

#8292 Let's Get This Day Started: Math   ©*Teacher Created Resources*

Name: _____

Plane and Solid Shapes

Teacher Directions: Read the page aloud to students. Talk about the differences between plane and solid shapes.

Plane shapes are flat.

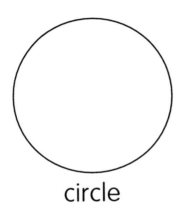

circle

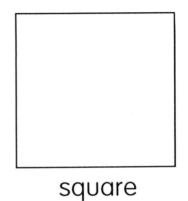

square

Solid shapes are **not** flat.

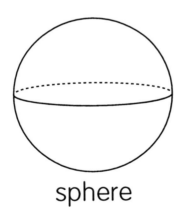

sphere

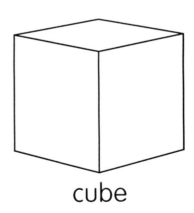

cube

Shapes are all around us!

sphere

cube

pyramid

cylinder

Geometry

PARTNER &
PRACTICE

Plane and Solid Shapes

Teacher Directions: Have students work with partners to color the plane shapes red and the solid shapes blue. Help students color the key first to ensure that they use the proper colors for each shape.

red = plane shapes   blue = solid shapes

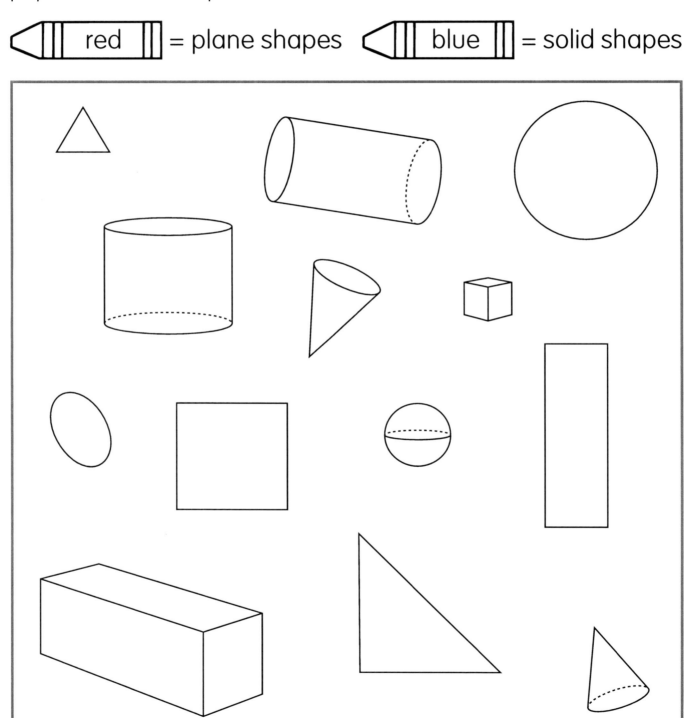

Name: _____

Plane and Solid Shapes

Teacher Directions: Have students find the shapes that are not solid and cross them out.

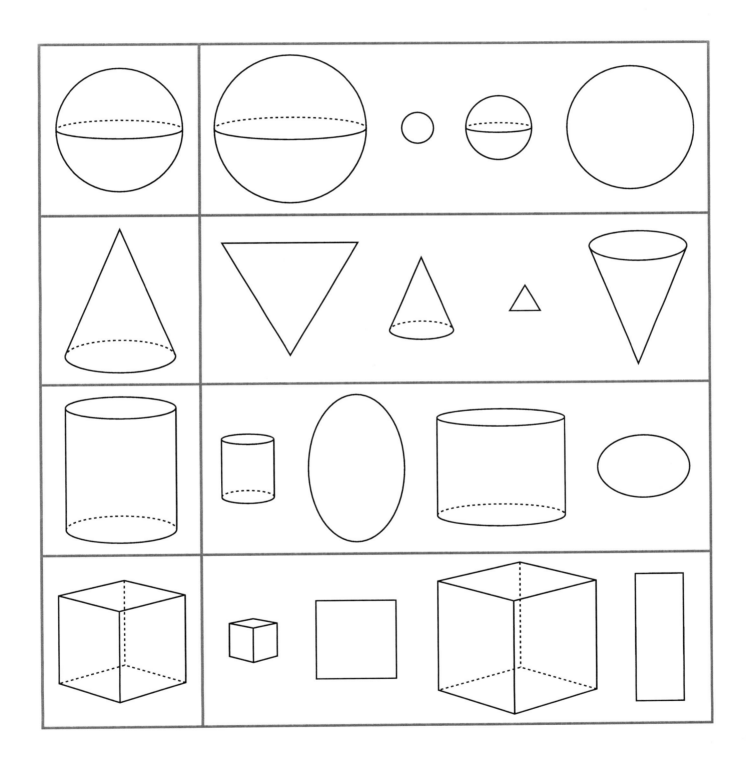

Name: _____

Plane and Solid Shapes

Teacher Directions: Have students think about the difference between plane shapes and solid shapes. Read aloud the directions and question to students.

Which shape is solid? Circle it.

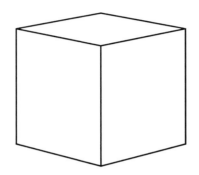

Draw a picture that shows what you learned about plane and solid shapes.

Name: _____

Comparing Shapes

Teacher Directions: Read the page aloud to students. Talk about all the different ways we can compare shapes.

Some shapes are bigger than others.

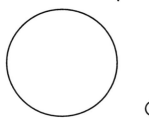

Some shapes are smaller than others.

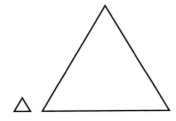

We can count how many sides they have.

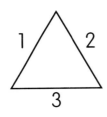

3 sides

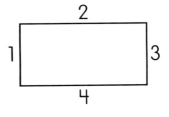

4 sides

We can say if they are plane or solid shapes.

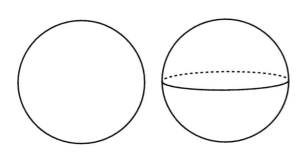

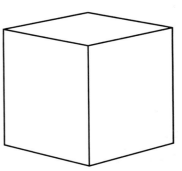

Name: _____

Comparing Shapes

Teacher Directions: Have students work with partners to color the correct answers. Read each sentence aloud for students.

Color the biggest circle.

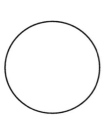 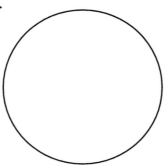

Color the smallest square.

  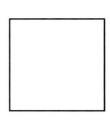

Color the shape that has the most sides.

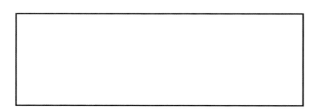 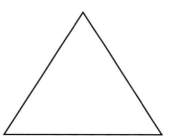

Color the shape that is solid.

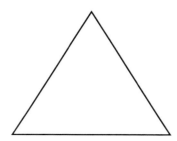 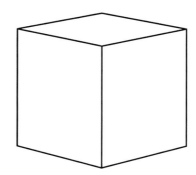

Name: _____

Comparing Shapes

Teacher Directions: Have students color the correct the answers. Read each sentence aloud for students.

Color the smallest triangle.

 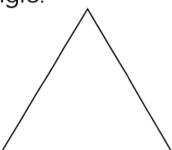 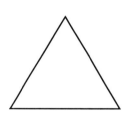

Color the biggest circle.

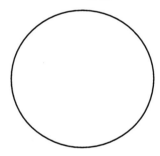 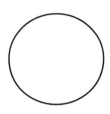

Color the shape that is plane.

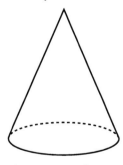 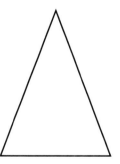

Color the shape that has the most sides.

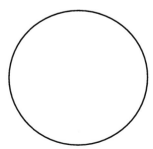 

Name: _____

Comparing Shapes

Teacher Directions: Have students think about all the different ways we can compare shapes. Read the directions aloud to students.

Draw a shape that has more sides than this.

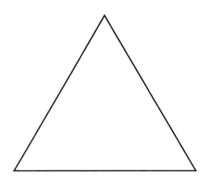

Draw a picture that shows what you learned about comparing shapes.